WITH ALL MY LOVE I HATE YOU

A Play

LYNDA MARCHAL

SAMUEL FRENCH

LONDON
NEW YORK TORONTO SYDNEY HOLLYWOOD

For
MR and MRS W. R. TITCHMARSH

CHARACTERS

Clare: A pathetic woman, who suffers from an inferiority complex. The loss of her child and her husband's indifference cause her to break down. Whilst at the clinic she works on her plan to destroy Julia and hopefully her husband, so her eventual meeting with Julia has been worked and calculated. Throughout the play she is aware of what she is doing, changing from pathos to anger to coaxing—and to hurting herself. The more hurt she feels, the better as it goads her towards the final climax and the end of the play

Julia: A clever, calculating woman, very attractive and calm. If Clare seems to have the leading hand, this is only because Julia is finding out how much Clare knows, why she is at her flat. Though she is far cleverer than Clare and could say and do more than she actually says and does, her guilt makes her listen—and walk straight into Clare's final trap

The action of the play passes in Julia's flat

Time – the present

WITH ALL MY LOVE I HATE YOU

Julia's flat. Lunchtime

It is an elegant, tastefully furnished business woman's flat. The lounge has all the other rooms leading off it, and the front door is beyond the kitchen

When the Curtain *rises Julia is discovered doing a crossword puzzle and eating a sandwich. There is a cup of coffee on the table in front of her. On the desk are a few photographs, including one of a boy which can be seen, but does not look obviously placed. There are also files, papers, and a telephone*

Julia is relaxed and not expecting anyone to call, but after a moment the front doorbell rings sharply three times. She looks up, folds the paper and picks up the coffee-cup. The bell rings again

Julia (*calling*) I'm coming.

The bell rings again

    Julia exits with the cup. The front door is heard to open

    (*Off*) Yes?

Clare (*off; her voice high-pitched and hysterical*) Thank God you were in. I have to talk to you.

Julia (*off; baffled*) I'm sorry . . .

Clare (*off*) Please, Julia, it's me—Clare, Clare Summerton. I have to talk to you, please let me come in.

Julia (*off*) Good heavens—why, yes, yes, of course.

Clare (*off*) You must think me quite mad coming to you like this, but I had no-one—you were the only person I could think of . . .

Julia (*off*) You'd better come in.

    Julia enters

This way.

Clare follows behind Julia. She wears a mink coat wrapped round her, a hat pulled down over her face and heavy dark glasses. She is very worked up and stands shaking a handkerchief clutched in her hands

You'd better sit down. I'll get you a drink. (*She goes to the drinks cabinet*) Gin?
Clare (*in a muffled voice*) Yes, yes, that's fine.
Julia Tonic and lemon?
Clare If you have some.
Julia I'm sure I do. (*She pours the drinks*) Do sit down.

Clare still stands

I'll get some ice.

Julia exits

Clare now seems to relax. She listens to Julia in the kitchen then slowly walks farther into the room. She stands taking in the room, then removes her hat and throws it on a chair. She begins to walk round the room, gets to the desk, is about to move away when she notices the photo of the little boy. She stares at it. Julia can be heard walking back towards the room. Clare sits at the desk and cries into her handkerchief

Julia enters with the drink

Julia (*handing Clare her glass*) Here we are.
Clare Thank God you were in. I don't know what I'd have done if you'd been out.
Julia Well, I wasn't. (*She sits*) Now, what's all the trouble? How can I help?

Clare hunches over, almost knocking her glasses off

Don't you think you'd manage a bit better if you took those awful glasses off?
Clare Yes, they are a bit ridiculous, aren't they? I must look a dreadful mess.

Julia I think you look marvellous—not that I can see very much of you.

Clare (*in a brittle voice*) That's very sweet of you, but I know what I look like. (*She gulps at her drink*) Oh, this is nice—thank you.

Julia Why don't you take your coat off and make yourself more comfortable?

Clare (*sharply*) No, I won't . . . (*She smiles*) Well, all right, yes, I will. (*She stands up and starts to remove her coat*)

Julia (*going to her*) I'll hang it up.

Clare (*clutching it*) No, please don't bother. (*She folds it over the chair. There is a pause*) This is a very nice room. I like it.

Julia Yes, it is very pleasant. It's light. I think that's what I like best about the whole flat—it's so . . .

Clare (*interrupting*) Yes. I've always liked nice airy rooms. They don't make you feel trapped. (*A pause*) Would you mind if I had another drink?

Julia No, of course not. (*She takes Clare's glass*)

Clare (*after a pause*) I must be an awful bother, barging in on you like this.

Julia (*carefully*) There hasn't been an accident, has there?

Clare Oh, no, nothing like that. I'm disturbing you?

Julia (*pouring a drink*) Not at all. I was just reading.

Clare I wouldn't want to interrupt anything. (*She goes and stands behind Julia*) You see, I found your letter.

Julia (*suddenly still*) Letter?

Clare Yes, the one you wrote after Susie—after the funeral. That's why I've come to you. (*She takes the glass*)

Julia (*sits, relieved*) I'm glad.

Clare (*after a pause; staring at the photo*) Who's that—the little boy?

Julia My son.

Clare (*shocked, but recovering quickly*) Oh, I didn't know about him. I didn't even know that you were . . .

Julia I'm not.

Clare Oh. Er—how old is he?

Julia Nearly seven.

Clare How nice. Does he live here with you?

Julia When he's not at school.

Clare What's his name?

Julia Robin.

Clare I didn't know. (*She walks away*) Has been a long time—
must be, what, nearly eight years?

Julia Yes, long time.

Clare (*sitting*) Have you lived here a long time?

Julia No, not all that long. Let me see, I moved in just before
I wrote to . . .

Clare (*not listening, pulling at her dress*) I've got fat, haven't I?
I can't seem to be able to lose it.

There is a pause

Clare I must have put on about two stone. . . .   } *speaking*
Julia How's Jerry? It's been such a long time . . . I'm } *together*

Clare I'm sorry. What did you say?

Julia Jerry. How is he?

Clare (*after drinking*) Oh—he's fine. Very well, very rich. (*She
drinks*)

Julia Do give him my love when you see him.

Clare Yes. Yes, I'll do that.

Julia (*after a pause*) Another drink?

Clare Just a small one. I'm not supposed to. I've got fat. Do you
think I've got fat?

Julia You look fine. (*She takes the glass and refills it*)

Clare Fine! (*She takes off the glasses. Her face is puffy and tired,
with deep rings beneath her over-made-up eyes*) Look at my
face. I used to be—wasn't I pretty? Now look at me.

Julia You're just tired. (*She hands Clare her drink*)

Clare (*taking the drink*) Am I? Perhaps—it's the drink that does
it, and I can't stop. I've tried—I've tried to, and I can't—
· *Christ!*

Julia Had you been drinking before you came here?

Clare Don't remember. (*Standing*) Why—heard rumours, have
you?

Julia No, of course not.

Clare You don't read the right papers. (*In a spoilt childish voice*)
Why have you never been to see me?

Julia I could ask the same of you.

Clare (*edging towards the photo*) True—true—I admire you. He's
good-looking.

Julia (*laughing*) Because he's good-looking?

Clare No, for having him on your own. I didn't know about him.
Julia Well, you wouldn't.
Clare (*sharply*) Why?
Julia We haven't seen each other.
Clare (*smiling*) No, of course not. (*She wanders across the room*) How many bedrooms?
Julia Two. Just Robin's and mine.
Clare That's nice. Cosy. You've never been to my—our—house, have you?
Julia No, no, I haven't. It must be very . . .
Clare Empty. It's an empty picture-book house with a gardener, a maid—we don't have a nanny any more.
Julia I was sorry—so very sorry. It was such a tragedy.
Clare Yes, so you said in your letter. (*She drains her glass*)
Julia (*after a pause*) Clare—why have you come here?
Clare (*shrugging*) I suppose I should have rushed in and slapped your face.
Julia What?
Clare Jerry would be amazed to see me now—so calm. I don't think he'd believe it.
Julia I don't understand.
Clare Oh, yes, you do.
Julia Have you found out something?
Clare Yes, Julia, I found out.

There is a pause. Julia stands awkwardly

Julia What am I supposed to say now?
Clare Oh, nothing. I just want you to know I'm perfectly sane— that the balance of my mind is not disturbed in any way.
Julia When did you find out?
Clare Find out what?
Julia How long have you known?
Clare Known what?
Julia (*angrily*) For Christ's sake, Clare, are you playing some kind of game?
Clare No, Julia, I'm not playing a game, just want to talk to you, that's all.
Julia But talk to me about what?
Clare My life. I want to talk about my life, and what it's been like since I last saw you and why I want to end it.

Julia Just stop it, Clare, and tell me what you want.

Clare To die. I want to die—but there has to be a reason for wanting to die, and I think you should know mine.

Julia But why me, Clare? (*She lights a cigarette*) Clare, just what have you found out?

Clare That you are, and have been for the past eight years, my husband's mistress.

Julia You're being ridiculous.

Clare Oh, am I? I'm standing here, talking, in full control of my emotions. I'm not screaming or crying. I know—of course I know. That's why I'm here, because I've found out—and I want to talk to you. I'm going to tell you why I'm going to die.

Julia Just stop all this talk of dying . . .

Clare (*grinning*) But that is the whole point. I want your help. You see, I can't do it by myself. Oh, I've tried, believe me I've tried—pills, slitting my wrists—you see . . . (*She pushes her arm under Julia's nose*) Only managed the one, then I got scared and ran for help. Never could stand the sight of blood. Failure—utter failure.

Julia Go away, Clare, please. I want you to leave.

Clare (*standing still*) You have no right to ask me to leave. You owe me . . .

Julia Owe? I owe you . . .

Clare (*strongly*) Yes—*owe*. You owe me a little of your time after what you have done to me.

Julia Clare, I've never done anything to you. You brought it on yourself. I know you're not well—you shouldn't have come here. Jerry's told me how ill you've been, and coming here won't help. It'll only make things worse.

Clare Oh, he told you, did he? Well, that was kind of him, considering it was the pair of you that helped put me into that place. But there's nothing wrong with me. I feel marvellous— and I'd like another drink.

Julia (*sighing*) Yes, of course. Clare, did you come by car?

Clare (*laughing*) Because, dear Julia, you've managed to get me sitting down calmly doesn't mean that I've finished, or that I'm going yet. Far from it. You've spent eight years moving and destroying me like a—little chess piece, and I am going to tell you what it's been like. I'm calm because I have no fight left, but you can be sure of one thing—I hate you—hate you both.

Julia I don't know what to say to you, Clare.

Clare Then let me talk, please. You do owe it to me.

Julia (*handing her a drink*) Yes.

Clare (*smiling*) Thank you. I didn't think I had any feelings left, but when I found out that it was you, and had been you all along, I realized that you'd never been my friend, that you'd never really liked me—and that hurt.

Julia Of course I was your friend.

Clare Be honest, Julia. You couldn't have been, because you loved him from the beginning like I did, but I was the one he married. (*She leans back*) Now, you're not a stupid woman. You knew he couldn't make love to a bank balance, he had to touch me, make love to me—(*she leans forward*)—and, Julia, he did love me—and after him I didn't need anyone else. I loved, really loved, for the first time in my life. No, I craved for him, and he knew it. You probably did, too. He must have talked about me, laughed about me, because he knew that he could get me to go down on my hands and knees and beg for him. Have you any idea what it is like—to be made to crawl to a man, and when that man is your husband, just to have him hold you, touch you. (*She laughs*) Oh God, even when you know there are plenty more fish in the sea it doesn't make any difference, does it? (*She flicks a look at Julia, then away again*)

Julia No—no, it doesn't.

Clare So I went on, I couldn't leave him, no matter what he did to me. I just went on wanting him, and as I'd never even had so much as a tiny hold I clung on, hoping, staying and staying. (*She stands*) Must have been because I'm so rich. (*She laughs*) He was the first thing I couldn't buy. (*She starts to pour more gin*) Can I help myself?

Julia Yes, do.

Clare (*adding ice and tonic*) I used to be so jealous of you two all those years ago. You were always immersed in some deep intellectual conversation.

Julia We were just students. Everyone was the same. Looking back, I don't think our conversation was all that . . .

Clare Oh, come off it. There was a *bit* of difference. I mean, you two were at the university and I was around the corner at the wee secretarial college. I was just like all the others—little dollies—until it got out whose daughter I was—then, whoopee, did I have a ball. Everyone wanted to know Clare.

Julia I really can't see the point of all this.

Clare Except Jerry, he didn't want to know—he never came near. Why?

Julia For heaven's sake—we were just old friends.

Clare Ah yes, I always forget you are *older* than me.

Julia Yes, I am, and we were just friends.

Clare (*nastily*) *Old* friends. You were in *love* with him.

Julia (*angrily*) Yes, it didn't make a bit of difference to you, though, did it.

Clare (*flinging her arms around Julia*) Oh, my darling, I'm sorry. I didn't mean to say that. I don't know why I even started talking about it. Please say you forgive me. I do need you. I've come to you because I do need you so much. You are my friend, my only friend. It's just that I have to get it all out of my system. You're right. I am childish. I'm stupid and I'm childish.

Julia (*moving away*) That's all right. You've had too much to drink. I'll make some coffee.

Clare I don't need any. (*Coaxing*) Ahh, Julia, please, now don't look moody. I haven't been very well, you know that. I need my friend. My psychiatrist said I need friends. Don't you turn from me, not you, I've no-one else. (*She puts down her glass*) I'm not drunk, nowhere near. Please sit down. Come on, please.

Julia sits. Clare for a fraction shows relief—Julia must not get away from her

(*Going to sit at Julia's feet*) Hey, you remember when we met— for the very first time. 'Course you do—in that awful church hall, the Rehearsal Room—(*she laughs*)—the amateur dramatics. Who would have thought my dreams would come true, when I read that I was cast opposite Jerry. God! I can remember reading that list over and over just in case there was a misprint. We played the lovers, remember? (*She looks up slyly*)

Julia Yes, I remember.

Clare (*hugging her knees*) I'd wait for that kiss scene, the only time in my life I was always on time—never late, not for one

.rehearsal, and he never even noticed me. He was always laughing and talking to everyone, and I was always hanging around hoping he'd ask me out. He just wasn't interested.

Julia Why don't you sit in a chair?

Clare When he kissed me I wanted him more than anything in the world. I wanted—(*she flings her arms up*)—wanted him to rip me open, tear me apart.

Julia Isn't that what you think he's done?

Clare (*deflated*) Yes—yes, he's done that all right.

Julia So?

Clare So when he asked me to marry him it was my fairy-tale come true.

Julia And you got what you wanted.

Clare Yes—and so did he—Daddy's money—and when he got that he changed.

Julia (*with a shrug*) You could have left him then.

Clare You don't leave what you haven't got. I was his wife, but —you don't wake up one morning and hate. It takes time, piece by piece they have to take your love away; year by year you learn to hate as all the love is chipped away. Sometimes a little love is put back, so you lose ground. (*She looks up at Julia*)

Julia What do you mean?

Clare Oh, he'd refuse to sleep with me—wouldn't even say good night. Then . . .

Julia Go on.

Clare (*leaning on Julia's knee*) Oh, he'd come into my room. I'd pretend to be asleep, but I always knew he was there because I was always waiting, listening. He'd stand at the doorway, I'd feel him looking at me. (*She touches Julia's knee*) He must have known how much he was hurting me, how much I wanted him. Slowly he'd pull the sheets from me, then he'd touch me. Strange how gentle he could be when he wanted—wanted to make love to me.

Julia gets up

Oh, I'm sorry. I'm upsetting you. I don't mean to.

Julia (*sarcastically*) Don't you? Isn't that what you've come here for, what you are trying to make me feel?

Clare (*going to her open-armed*) I don't want you to feel anything.

How can I hurt you—you who have so much more than I—
more than I ever had? And you have his son—I have nothing.
(*She moves away*) Now I don't want you to feel sorry for me—
not that. It's just that you know why I took so much. You
waited nights, when you knew he was with me, knew he was
making love to me. You knew about those nights, didn't you?

Julia (*upset*) Yes, I knew.

Clare (*hugging her*) Of course you did. (*She moves away with her
back to Julia, smiling*) That's why I've come to you. You know
all about me.

Julia What do you want, Clare? Why are you telling me all this?
I don't want to know.

Clare (*burying her head in the arm of a chair*) He's asked for a
divorce.

Julia Divorce?

Clare (*weeping*) He's going to prove that I'm insane, mentally
unstable—and it's not true. You know that—that I've been
ill, but that was because of Susie—the accident. The shock
made me collapse. But there's nothing wrong with me. (*She
bangs the chair*) It was depression—just depression.

Julia I didn't know.

Clare 'Course you did—everyone knew they took me away at
the funeral.

Julia No—about the divorce.

Clare (*stopping weeping*) You didn't know?

Julia We talked about it, of course, but . . .

Clare (*springing up*) Oh, he just doesn't want to drag you through
all his lies. He wants to keep your name out of it. You will
help me, though, won't you? You won't let him take me to
court. (*She clings on to Julia's arm*) I couldn't bear to have to
remember it all again. I couldn't go through all that again.

Julia He wouldn't do that.

Clare (*in a fury*) Oh, yes, he would. He *hates* me. All those lies
he spread about me at the inquest—and they *were* lies—he
wanted me to break. He wanted me to collapse.

Julia Now come on, he doesn't hate you.

Clare (*screaming*) How the hell do you know? But wait—just you
wait. When he gets rid of me it'll be your turn. When I'm out
of the way he'll start on you.

Julia (*moving away*) I'm not going to listen to you.

Clare smiles behind Julia's back

You're overwrought. What on earth is the point of all this? Whatever I say won't be enough. You need a friend—of course you do—but not me. I'm the wrong person to help you. You shouldn't have come to me.

Clare (*grabbing her arm*) How can you love someone like—how can you love him when he treats me like this? But think, he'll be rid of me, so why is he keeping the divorce a secret? So he won't have to marry you—right?

Julia Oh, Clare, really . . ..

Clare (*nastily*) You're so sure of his love, aren't you. There's not a tiny seed of doubt in the "oh-so-together" mind of yours.

Julia (*angrily*) And you are so sure he never loved you, aren't you—so sure he hates you.

Clare What do you mean?

Julia Oh, Clare, I was jealous of you. I knew he was going to marry you. You don't really think I planned my life like this, do you? The eternal mistress? He married you because he loved you. He wanted you. And believe me, no matter how much I cried —how much I begged him not—it was you he wanted.

Clare No, that's not true. He married me for my money. That's not true.

Julia All right, it's not true. I don't really care. All I know is I love and I've always loved him. Can't you see? If I'd ever had any real strength I'd have left years ago. But I couldn't. I've always been here waiting, and whatever hurt I felt when he left me to go to you I never showed. I had no right—you were his wife.

Clare (*whipping round on her*) Then why wouldn't you let him be my husband—always lurking in the background like some bloody vulture. You never gave my marriage a chance.

Julia Believe me, I did.

Clare (*screaming*) *And believe me you didn't!* I used to rack my brains. Why—why didn't it work? At times he seemed to love me, care for me. Then, just like that, he'd change, he'd resent me. *Why?* Because he'd just come from you—*you*, always waiting—waiting with open arms. You destroyed my marriage —my family . . .

Julia *What?* Destroyed what—did you say?

Clare (*crying*) When Susie was born we were happy, and he wouldn't have left me alone then.

Julia Wouldn't he?

Clare (*out of control*) No, he wouldn't—but you were still around, and my God what a weapon you had—his son! It was your fault I started drinking. Your fault . . .

Julia Oh, and how did you work that out?

Clare You—you—you enticed him away from me. When I was fat and ugly and pregnant with his child you were here—screwing my husband.

Julia For Christ's sake, Clare, he wasn't even sure if it was his child.

Clare freezes. She turns to Julia, walks slowly to her, and swipes at her face

Clare You bitch, how dare you say that!

There is a pause. Julia holds her face

Julia I'm sorry, I shouldn't have said that. I'm sorry. Dear God, Clare, look what you're doing. Go away.

Clare (*calmly, her hands clenched*) I haven't finished yet.

Julia Well, you might as well know one thing. We were going to tell you—just before you became pregnant—about Robin, about me—everything.

Clare (*spitting out the words*) My God, I bet my being in the club must have made you sit up. I bet that was a shock. What did he tell you—that he never touched me, that we slept in different rooms? (*She laughs*) I am sorry, if I'd known I'd have had an abortion—made things easier for you.

Julia I'm sorry. I asked for that.

Clare Yes, you did. He loved her, adored her, and we were happy.

Julia Yes, of course he loved her.

Clare (*her control going*) Yes—yes, and if you hadn't always been around waiting, if the accident, if Susie, if . . .

Julia Yes . . .

Clare That was a lucky break for you, wasn't it—the accident.

Julia That's a terrible thing to say—or did you hate her as well?

Clare (*turning, trying to shrug it off*) Sometimes I was jealous of her—his love for her . . . (*She stands, unable to speak*)

Julia How did she die, Clare?

Clare (*quietly*) You read the papers, don't you?

Julia Papers—but I'd like to hear your version.

Clare It was an accident.

Julia Was it?

Clare She ran out into the street and was run over.

Julia Tell me the truth.

Clare (*in a brittle voice, heading for the gin bottle*) Hasn't he told you? I killed her. "You killed her, you killed my baby." That's what he says. That's what he tells all his friends.

kulia No, he . . .

Clare He didn't even come to see me once in the Home, and when they let me go he didn't even come and collect me. He sent the car. (*She pours a drink*) He'd moved most of his things out, taken a flat somewhere, never could find out where, he's very good at hiding things. (*She looks at Julia*) 'Course, he still had to come home occasionally. He still needed me to sign the odd cheque. He hardly spoke to me—just looked through me if I talked to him, and if I went to touch him he'd move away. I don't know which was worse, his not being there, or his being there and not even . . . (*She sits*) They let me forget for a while in the Home. The pain went away—drugs, I suppose, but I was calm. Her face didn't follow me. I could sleep and not see her, wake up and not think about her, and there they told me over and over—it was an accident—it wasn't my fault.

Julia Why didn't you leave him? Why did you go back there?

Clare Because somewhere deep inside I still had a little love left, and I needed, not much—but I hoped he'd help me, hoped he'd come home.

Julia Did he come home—help you?

Clare You should know. He must have been here with you. I just wanted him to listen to me, Julia. I wanted to get down on my knees in front of him and swear before God on that day I was stone cold sober.

Julia (*moved*) Oh, Clare . . .

Clare Now I know why he never came. He had you, and you had his son. He didn't even need to think of me. But, Julia, we were happy. He'd even started to bring work home at week-ends so that he could be with us both.

Julia Yes, he loved her very much.

Clare (*sitting very still, her eyes staring*) On that week-end I remember the sun. It was a lovely day. We had a big drive-way: his car, the Bentley, was parked behind mine and I asked him to move it. I noticed that the keys were in the ignition, but —I called again, I called three times. He always hated me driving it. Susie was on the lawn. She could only just crawl. I decided to move it.. . . .

Julia Don't go on.

Clare I walked around the car—she must have crawled then—it was automatic. I can't even remember if I put it into gear. It all happened so quickly—the car seemed to leap backwards. I got flustered, thought I'd better ask Jerry to move it after all. I walked up the path, turned to see if she was all right . . . She died instantly. That's what they said—instantly, without so much as a cry.

Julia Clare . . .

Clare "Look what you've done to my child, you drunken bitch." Not ours—mine. (*She shrugs*) They took me away shortly after. I went into the Home. I never realized that one could feel so much pain. (*She pauses*) I wanted him to understand, Julia, needed him to help me—and he never so much as held my hand.

Julia Please, I don't want to hear any more . . .

Clare (*brightly*) But I haven't got to the best bit yet. You're not expecting anyone, are you? Is someone coming?

Julia No, but I . . .

Clare Oooh, come on, let's get drunk together. (*She wraps her arms round Julia*)

Julia I think . . .

Clare Come on, just another drinkie.

Julia It would be better if you . . .

Clare (*shrieking*) Go! Go! You want me to go?

Julia I was going to say—coffee.

Clare (*giggling*) Oh, I am sorry. What a temper—jumping to conclusions like that. Are you getting frightened of me?

Julia (*moving away*) No, of course not. Why should I?

Clare Oh, no reason. Do you feel sorry for me?

Julia I don't know what I feel. You keep muddling me, and I think you're getting very drunk. I think it would be best if you did go.

Clare (*smiling*) I used to plot how to kill you.

Julia (*going to get Clare's coat*) I'll call you a cab.

Clare (*grabbing the coat*) Leave that alone. (*She smiles*) Night after night I used to plot. Shall I tell you some of my methods? Would you like to hear?

Julia No. I'll call a taxi, then make coffee.

Clare I've got a gun in my pocket.

Julia Stop playing games.

Clare Don't you believe me? I was going to sneak up behind you and when you weren't looking shoot you in the back. (*She digs Julia*) But then I thought I'd prefer to shoot you in the face so that you could see me do it. (*She grins*) Where are you going?

Julia To telephone. You'd better go home.

Clare I'm not ready yet. (*She hops on one foot*) Another way was ramming you with my mini. You'd be splattered all over the pavement and I'd be sitting watching—waiting for you to die.

Julia dials a number on the telephone at the desk

You'd be begging me to help you——

Julia (*on the telephone*) Hello? . . . Julia Gardener here, number twenty-two . . .

Clare —crawling in the gutter. (*She sighs*) But I went off that idea, too. You're so bloody clever you'd probably jump over the mini.

Julia (*into the telephone*) Yes, Kensington, right away.

Clare (*picking up the photo of the boy*) Now, if I'd known about him I'd have had a marvellous time. I didn't know about him.

Julia (*into the telephone*) Ten minutes? Yes, that's fine. Thank you. You know the address . . . Yes, thank you. (*She hangs up*)

Clare That would have been a good way—kidnap your son and make him have a accident like Susie.

Julia Give me that.

Clare This? Here, have it. (*She throws the photo at Julia's feet*)

Julia I think you'd better get your things together. The taxi will be here any moment.

Clare (*grinning*) Getting rid of me, Julia?

Julia (*becoming angry*) I never asked you to come here. I've sat most of the afternoon listening to your abuse, your crude-

ness. Why? Because I do feel sorry for you. I do feel a certain
amount of guilt. I know you've been ill mentally, so I've stood
a lot more than I need to—but don't go too far.

Clare (*angrily*) Just what in hell do you mean by that "ill mentally"? There's nothing wrong with me.

Julia Isn't there? Of course you're ill—you've been brooding
in the house for weeks alone—drinking, hating—but don't
think that you alone have the right to those feelings. I've had
my share. Don't think I don't know what it's like to hate, I've
hated you, and you know damn well I have. You took Jerry
away from me in the beginning. I warned you, tried to tell
you that I couldn't let him go, but you wouldn't listen, and
you didn't care how much pain you caused me. Don't think
I don't know what he's like, what he is. He's a bastard—a
selfish, egotistical bastard—everything you've hinted at I've
known already. You can't touch me.

Clare My, my, what an onslaught. I never came for that!

Julia Of course you did. What else have you been trying to do?
Turn me against him by making me pity you. You've been
trying to make me hate him as much as you do, but you can't.
I'd never let go. We've wanted to be together for years, but
you'd never let him go, would you? You clung on. How many
times has he asked for a divorce? How many?

Clare He's never asked me for a divorce before now.

Julia (*shouting*) You're lying. You've been lying to me all
afternoon. You almost ruined his career with your lies. Read
about you? 'Course I've bloody read about you. Who hasn't?
"Drunken bitch" may have been crude, but by God *it was
true!*

*Clare stares, tries to control herself, but sits hunched. Throughout
the rest of Julia's speech she seems to crumple like a rag doll*

Oh God, Clare, can't you see what you're doing? You're
making me say things I don't want to—raking up the past. It's
better left alone. We'll only hurt each other. (*She goes to Clare*)
Clare, I'm asking you, begging you—leave us alone, let us be
together. (*She takes Clare's hand*) Try to face facts, no matter
how painful. Jerry and I love each other. We always have
done. And he loves his son. We're a family. You lost him to
me a long time ago. Let me have him—please.

Clare (*standing*) All right!

Julia What?

Clare Ever since I found out it was you I knew I didn't stand a chance. "Darling, I'll be home late. Dinner in the oven. Sorry I'm not in bed."

Julia looks puzzled

Such an innocent little note, but I found it, and I kept it and I put it in my drawer along with my silk scarves and the sweet letters about Susie—and your letter of condolence and the innocent note matched. It all fitted into place. It had to be you.

Julia I see . . .

Clare (*taking the gun out of her pocket*) Do you?

Julia Clare!

Clare You said I had reason to hate. Don't be frightened. I've waited for this moment for a very long time.

Julia backs

No, please don't be frightened. I won't use it on you. It's for me.

Julia Clare, Clare, you don't know what you're doing.

Clare Oh, yes, I do. I've worked it out in every little detail.

Julia (*trying to keep calm*) Give me the gun.

Clare (*smiling and releasing the safety catch*) Here—take it.

Julia *What?*

Clare The gun—take it, but be careful. It's not a toy, it's loaded.

Julia What?

Clare Come on, take it. Come on, put out your hand and take it.

Julia You'll take your hand away.

Clare No, I won't. Come on—take it.

Julia (*slowly reaching out her hand and taking the gun*) Clare . . .

Clare There, you see?

Julia But why—why did you let me take it?

Clare Simple. I want you to kill me.

Julia Kill you?

Clare I can't do it by myself, and you never know, you might need it later.

Julia What—what do you mean?

Clare Can't you guess, Julia?

Julia (*whispering*) Dear God, Clare, what have you done?

Clare (*brightly and very quickly*) I've been extremely clever. You see, at ten-thirty this morning I phoned my beloved husband at his office and I told him that I knew all about you and that it put a slightly different slant on the divorce. 'Course, he didn't believe me. Then I said that if he wasn't at the house within half an hour I'd do a little business of my own. I still hold most of the shares. (*She laughs*) Well, you can imagine, he must have left that office in a panic.

Julia (*pointing the gun at Clare and beginning to back*) Well—go on.

Clare (*strongly, quietly*) The house was empty, empty as it has always been for me, and I waited as I had always waited . . .

Julia (*backing*) Go on.

Clare I could hear him running up the path. It's gravel, you can hear very clearly, and I'd left the door open.

Julia Don't come any closer. Stay where you are.

Clare (*stopping*) I was on the stairs where Susie used to hide. It's dark. He couldn't see me, but I could—I could see him. He called my name—once, twice, three times. I stood up— still he didn't see me.

Julia What have you done?

Clare moves forward

Stay away from me. You didn't—you . . .

Clare (*moving forward again*) Phone him, Julia—phone him. See if he returned to the office—but you're going to have a long wait. (*She moves again*) He's dead, he's dead, Julia. I've killed him. (*She lifts her coat as if to move against Julia*)

Julia moves backwards in a panic, but she is up against the desk. Her arm jolts and the gun fires as Clare says "I've killed him". Clare falls without expression, being killed instantly at that close range. She lies at Julia's feet

Julia (*staring*) Oh, my God—no, no—I didn't mean it—it went off—get up, dear God, Clare, get up. (*She cries, frightened, the gun still in her hand. Then, still crying, she goes to the phone and dials*)

Voice: Hello—Jerry Summerton Property Investments . . .

Julia (*speaking into the telephone with difficulty*) Please—please— Jerry—is he there?

Voice Oh, hello—just one moment and I'll put you through.
  (*The telephone clicks*)
Jerry's Voice: Hello—hello—hello . . .

Julia lets the receiver fall from her hand, as—

the CURTAIN *falls*

FURNITURE AND PROPERTY LIST

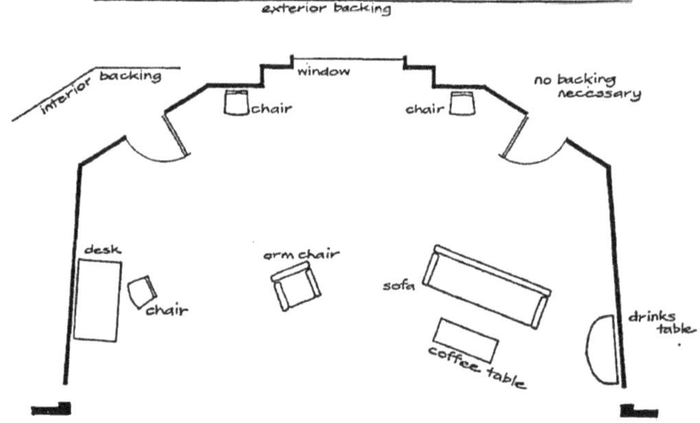

On stage: Settee. *On it:* newspaper opened at crossword puzzle, pencil
          Coffee-table. *On it:* cup of coffee, sandwich on plate, cigarettes, ashtray, lighter
          Desk. *On it:* writing materials, telephone, framed photograph including one of small boy, files, papers
          Drinks table. *On it:* various bottles and glasses, including gin, tonic water
          Desk chair
          2 small chairs
          Armchair
          Carpet
          Window curtains

Off stage: Bowl of ice (**Julia**)
          Gun (**Clare**)

Personal: **Clare:** handkerchief, dark glasses

LIGHTING PLOT

Property fittings required: nil
  A sitting-room

To open: General effect of afternoon light
No cues

EFFECTS PLOT

Cue 1   As Curtain rises   (Page 1)
         Doorbell rings three times

Cue 2   Julia picks up coffee-cup   (Page 1)
         Doorbell rings

Cue 3   **Julia:** "I'm coming."   (Page 1)
         Doorbell rings